Pharrell
WILLIAMS

Joanne Mattern

Mitchell Lane
PUBLISHERS
P.O. Box 196
Hockessin, Delaware 19707
Visit us on the web: www.mitchelllane.com

Mitchell Lane
PUBLISHERS

Printing   1   2   3   4   5   6   7   8   9

Blue Banner Biographies

5 Seconds of Summer
Abby Wambach
Adele
Alicia Keys
Allen Iverson
Ashanti
Ashlee Simpson
Ashton Kutcher
Avril Lavigne
Blake Lively
Blake Shelton
Bow Wow
Brett Favre
Britney Spears
Bruno Mars
CC Sabathia
Carrie Underwood
Chris Brown
Chris Daughtry
Christina Aguilera
Ciara
Clay Aiken
Cole Hamels
Condoleezza Rice
Corbin Bleu
Daniel Radcliffe
David Ortiz
David Wright
Derek Jeter
Drew Brees
Dwayne Wade
Eminem
Eve
Fergie
Flo Rida
Gwen Stefani
Hope Solo

Ice Cube
Ja Rule
Jamie Foxx
Jason Derulo
Jay-Z
Jennifer Hudson
Jennifer Lopez
Jessica Simpson
JJ Watt
J. K. Rowling
Joe Flacco
John Legend
Justin Berfield
Justin Timberlake
Kanye West
Kate Hudson
Katy Perry
Keith Urban
Kelly Clarkson
Kenny Chesney
Ke$ha
Kevin Durant
Kristen Stewart
Lady Gaga
Lance Armstrong
Leona Lewis
Lil Wayne
Lionel Messi
Lindsay Lohan
LL Cool J
Luke Bryan
Ludacris
Mariah Carey
Mario
Mary J. Blige
Mary-Kate and Ashley Olsen
Megan Fox

Miguel Tejada
Mike Trout
Nancy Pelosi
Natasha Bedingfield
Nicki Minaj
One Direction
Orianthi
Orlando Bloom
P. Diddy
Peyton Manning
Pharrell Williams
Pink
Pit Bull
Prince William
Queen Latifah
Rihanna
Robert Downey Jr.
Robert Pattinson
Ron Howard
Russell Wilson
Sean Kingston
Selena
Shakira
Shia LaBeouf
Shontelle Layne
Soulja Boy Tell 'Em
Stephenie Meyer
Taylor Swift
T.I.
Timbaland
Tim McGraw
Tim Tebow
Toby Keith
Usher
Vanessa Anne Hudgens
Will.i.am
Zac Efron

Library of Congress Cataloging-in-Publication Data
Mattern, Joanne, 1963–
Pharrell Williams / by Joanne Mattern.
    pages cm. — (Blue banner biographies)
Includes bibliographical references and index.
ISBN 978-1-68020-087-4 (library bound)
1. Williams, Pharrell—Juvenile literature. 2. Rap musicians—United States—Biography—Juvenile literature. I. Title.
ML3930.W55M37 2016
782.421649092--dc23
[B]
                                                                2015012927
eBook ISBN: 978-1-68020-088-1

ABOUT THE AUTHOR: Joanne Mattern is the author of many nonfiction books for children. She especially enjoys writing biographies and has profiled many celebrities for Mitchell Lane Publishers, including One Direction, Ludacris, Selena, Jennifer Hudson, and Blake Lively. As a fan of many different styles of music, she especially enjoys writing about artists such as Pharrell Williams. Mattern lives in New York State with her husband, four children, and several pets.

PUBLISHER'S NOTE: The following story has been thoroughly researched and to the best of our knowledge represents a true story. While every possible effort has been made to ensure accuracy, the publisher will not assume liability for damages caused by inaccuracies in the data and makes no warranty on the accuracy of the information contained herein. This story has not been authorized or endorsed by Pharrell Williams.

Blue Banner Biography

Pharrell Williams, hip-hop star and judge on the hit show The Voice, electrifies the crowd at an iHeart Radio concert.

Twenty-four Hours of "Happy"

In 2013 people were feeling happy. The reason was a catchy song from the movie *Despicable Me 2*. Sung by Pharrell Williams, the popularity of the song "Happy" soon exploded beyond the movie to become one of the hottest songs of the year.

Williams and a directing team called We Are From Los Angeles (WAFLA) came up with the idea to turn "Happy" into a twenty-four-hour interactive video. The idea had never been done before, and WAFLA was eager to try. When they heard Williams' song, they knew they had just the right elements to create their historic video.

WAFLA sent a proposal for the video to i am OTHER, the company that Williams launched in 2012. "WAFLA had always wanted to do a twenty-four-hour video and they were waiting for the right project," Mimi Valdes, the vice president of i am OTHER explained to www.fastcocreate. com. "They sent their proposal, and I remember I had to close my computer before I finished reading because I had this overwhelming feeling of excitement, which Pharrell obviously shared. It felt big. We had absolutely no idea how we were going to pull it off, but we instinctively felt it was too good an idea not to work."

The project was complicated. The video repeated the song over and over — 360 times — and it showed people dancing and expressing their happiness. Thousands of people auditioned to be in the video. "We wanted as diverse a group as possible — all ages, all ethnicities, all types," said Valdes. "Our choices were based mostly on personality — people who looked like they'd have fun on camera." Many celebrities, including Jimmy Kimmel, Tyler the Creator, Kelly Osbourne, and Steve Carell also appeared in the film, along with several of the Minions from *Despicable Me 2*. WAFLA spent weeks figuring out where to film and they traveled all over Los Angeles and its surrounding areas to find the right shooting locations.

> *"I'm not interested in perfection. It's boring," Williams explained. "Some of my favorite moments are accidental."*

The video took eleven days to film, including two days dedicated to Pharrell's performances. Williams performs the song once every hour, for a total of twenty-four performances. Each hour also features fourteen other performances. All the performers — four hundred people — were filmed in one take, and any mistakes they made were left in the video. Williams especially enjoyed the bloopers and live action. "I'm not interested in perfection. It's boring," he explained. "Some of my favorite moments are accidental." To make the video interactive, a clock was added to allow viewers to click on any time to see the

Williams' music for the movie Despicable Me 2 *made everyone "Happy." Here Williams, composer Heitor Pereira, and Mike Knobloch of Universal Pictures arrive at the premiere of* Despicable Me 2 *at the Gibson Amphitheatre in Universal City, California.*

specific performances at that time in the twenty-four hour video.

"Twenty-Four Hours of Happy" became a huge hit on YouTube, where it has been viewed millions of times. People watch the video straight through or they watch their favorite segments. Hearing the upbeat, jazzy rhythm and perky melody and lyrics, "Clap along if you feel like a room without a roof / Clap along if you feel like happiness is the truth," brought even more happiness to viewers. And that is something that Williams is proud of. Williams has spent his career trying new things and working to empower other people to follow their feelings and also try new things. His talent and fearlessness have earned Williams success in his career.

Williams was just one of the artists honoring legendary performer *Stevie Wonder* at the Stevie Wonder: Songs In The Key Of Life: An All-Star GRAMMY Salute *at the Nokia Theatre in Los Angeles on February 10, 2015.*

Discovering Music

Pharrell Williams was born in Virginia Beach, Virginia, on April 5, 1973. His parents are Pharaoh and Carolyn Williams. Pharrell's mother is a teacher and his father is a handyman. Pharrell has two brothers, Cato and Psolomon, who are a lot younger than he is. He also has two half brothers named Pharaoh and David.

Williams lived in a poor and tough neighborhood in Virginia Beach. Most of the young people in his neighborhood had limited lives with no future. Pharrell later spoke about the neighborhood to the *London Evening Standard*, "You have to understand that the world I grew up in was not one of high expectations. No one told us when we were young to be ambitious . . . If you didn't die in your twenties, you'd probably end up in prison or live a life of drugs."

Pharaoh and Carolyn Williams wanted a better life for their children. When Williams was seven years old the family moved to the suburbs. One of the best things about the move was how it exposed Pharrell to many different types of music. He told the radio station hitz.fm, "We lived across the street from a biker group . . . they played a lot of rock 'n' roll . . . Meanwhile in my house my mom and dad are playing Earth, Wind & Fire, but on the radio they are playing Rick James and Queen. I never really lost that." Williams believes that hearing so many different kinds of music, including rock, funk, pop, and disco, inspired him to mix different musical styles as an entertainer.

> *Williams believes that hearing so many different kinds of music, including rock, funk, pop, and disco, inspired him to mix different musical styles as an entertainer.*

Williams was able to learn more about music in school. He learned to play the drums and keyboards. In seventh grade Williams attended a summer band camp, and he met a boy named Chad Hugo. Hugo played the tenor saxophone. Although the two boys went to different schools, they discovered that they both played in marching bands. They became best friends and formed a band. Hugo later told VH1 that Williams would come to his house after school and they would make music in Hugo's garage. "Pharrell would come up with hooks and beats. We had the cheapest keyboards ever."

Education was important to Williams' family, especially to his mother, who is a teacher; however, Williams was just an average student. After he graduated from Princess Anne High School, Williams made it clear that he did not want to go to college. Surprisingly, Carolyn Williams did not get upset when Williams decided to skip college. She understood that it was the right choice for her oldest son. Years later she described Williams as a "creative, out-of-the-box thinker" to *Coastal Virginia* magazine.

Williams and Hugo already had an idea about what they wanted to do, and a school talent show gave them a great opportunity. During high school the two boys and their friends Shae Haley and Mike Etheridge formed a band called The Neptunes. They entered a high school talent show at Williams' school. Music producer Teddy Riley owned a studio next door to the school and came over to see the show. Riley had worked with some of the top hip-hop artists of the 1990s, including Bobby Brown and Al B. Sure. When he saw The Neptunes perform, he knew immediately that the group had talent.

After the show, Riley spoke to Williams and asked him to write some song lyrics. Williams came up with a rap verse that was used in a song called "Rump Shaker" by Wrecks-N-Effect. The song became a huge hit and Williams' first professional effort paid off.

Over the next few years, Williams wrote more music. He also learned how to create beats, produce music, and sing background vocals. Williams' road to the top was not easy. Many people felt that Williams and Hugo were too nerdy and did not have the right look to be hip-hop stars. Hugo told VH1 that when he and Williams entered recording studios, no one believed that they were there to make music. "They would be asking me where to order the best pizza," Hugo said. "I guess they're not used to seeing an Asian making music. But I'm just here to get people's heads bobbing . . . At the end of the day, your music speaks for itself."

Superstar recording artists Pharrell Williams, Jay Z, and Kanye West share a moment at the 57th Annual Grammy Awards at the Staples Center in Los Angeles, California, on February 8, 2015.

From Neptunes to N.E.R.D.s

*I*n the 1990s, Williams and Hugo began to enjoy success producing songs as The Neptunes. Several songs they produced became big hits on radio stations that played hip-hop, urban, and pop music. By 2000, they were producing some of the most popular songs on the radio.

A music producer often writes the songs, is responsible for how the song is recorded, decides what effects are used in the recording studio, and is responsible for how the finished song sounds. Many music producers stay behind the scenes, but Williams had other ideas. Because he was a talented writer and singer, he was often asked to write and perform on the records he produced. He even appeared in a few music videos. People liked his good looks, his voice, and his stylish presence. Soon Williams became known as someone more than a behind-the-scenes producer; he was also a performer.

In 2001, Britney Spears was one of the most popular singers in the music industry. One of the highlights of Williams' career was watching Spears perform her new song, "I'm a Slave 4 U" on the *MTV Video Music Awards*.

Williams told VH1 that it was one of the proudest moments of his life. He explained that the song "wasn't just our production. Those were my lyrics and everything . . . That was my moment . . . We made it."

Britney Spears wasn't the only star Williams and Hugo produced. They also created songs for stars such as Jay-Z, Usher, Justin Timberlake, and No Doubt. In 2002, The Neptunes won the Producer of the Year Award at the Source Awards and the Producers of the Year Award at the *Billboard* Music Awards.

> *Pharrell explained that the song "wasn't just our production. Those were my lyrics and everything . . . That was my moment . . . We made it."*

Williams and Hugo enjoyed producing, but they wanted to do more. They wanted to write and perform other music besides hip-hop. Williams and Hugo teamed up with Shae Haley and formed a band called N.E.R.D. The name stands for No One Ever Really Dies. N.E.R.D.'s music combines hip-hop and alternative rock. On the band's website, Williams explained the difference between The Neptunes and N.E.R.D. "The Neptunes are who we are and N.E.R.D. is what we do. It's our life."

N.E.R.D. released its first album, *In Search Of,* in 2001. At first, the album was only released in Europe. Williams and his bandmates weren't happy with the sound of the album, so they re-recorded it before they released it to the world in 2002. The album was a big hit and several songs made it to the Top Forty charts in the United States. *In Search Of* sold over five hundred thousand copies, and earned N.E.R.D. a gold record.

In 2003, Williams was ready to try something new. He released a solo single called "Frontin'." The song featured hip-hop superstar Jay-Z and was a hit on the radio. Next The Neptunes released an album called *The Neptunes Presents . . . Clones*. The album was also a hit, debuting at number one on the *Billboard* 200 chart.

In 2004, N.E.R.D. took the spotlight when they released the album *Fly or Die*. The title expressed Williams' feelings about looking on the bright side of life. "It's either fly or die; be optimistic or wither away into nothing. That should be everybody's motto in life. Go for it. If you don't go for it, you're gonna lose it."

Audiences loved *Fly or Die*. The album earned a gold record and was listed on the Top Ten on the *Billboard* 200 chart. The album's success gave the band the courage to play live onstage for the first time. Although the band had played in studios many times, they had never played to a live audience. Hugo explained on n-e-r-d.com that playing live was "more honest" and a way for people to see another side of the band. People loved the idea and Williams and his music became more popular than ever—but the best was yet to come.

> "It's either fly or die; be optimistic or wither away into nothing. That should be everybody's motto in life. Go for it. If you don't go for it, you're gonna lose it."

Every year, the iHeart Radio Jingle Ball concerts feature the hottest artists in contemporary music. On December 12, 2014, Pharrell Williams shared the stage with Gwen Stefani at Madison Square Garden in New York City.

CHAPTER 4

Success in Many Fields

Williams released his first solo album, *In My Mind*, in 2006. Williams had worked on the album for many months, but it was hard to find time to complete the album since Williams and The Neptunes were busy producing songs for other artists. Williams told MTV that he managed to squeeze in work on his album around his other responsibilities. "When I'm in the studio working on different people's sessions, in between sessions and before they get there, I work on tracks."

Creating songs for his albums while working for other artists paid off. Williams was producing a song for Gwen Stefani when he mentioned his solo work. Stefani asked to hear Williams' song. She liked the track so much that she insisted on working on Williams' music instead of her own. Together they recorded "Can I Have It Like That?" featured on the album *In My Mind*. The song was a success.

In 2005, Williams was recognized for something other than his musical style. His fashion style was in the spotlight. *Esquire* magazine named him 2005's Best Dressed Man in the World on its annual Best Dressed List. According to

Esquire, the list included people who were "the most innovative, never-trendy, and always perfectly clad-for-the-occasion individuals." Williams was honored to receive the title, but he didn't take it too seriously. He later told MTV that his fashion was "about comfort and flow. It's never about whether I'm the best-dressed guy in the room . . . Things just need to fit naturally."

> **Pharrell later told MTV that his fashion was "about comfort and flow. It's never about whether I'm the best-dressed guy in the room . . . Things just need to fit naturally."**

Even though he wasn't that impressed with being named the Best Dressed Man in the World, Williams had an interest in fashion. He joined forces with famous Japanese designer Tomoaki Nagao (aka Nigo) in 2005 to produce his own clothing lines. One line is named Billionaire Boys Club and the other is called Ice Cream. Both lines feature casual clothing, such as T-shirts, jackets, jeans, and accessories. Ice Cream also designs colorful cake-and-ice cream-inspired sneakers and other footwear.

Williams did not forget his first love. Between 2006 and 2009 Williams worked with Madonna, Beyoncé, Britney Spears, The Hives, Maroon 5, Jennifer Lopez, and Shakira. He also continued his production work with The Neptunes, working with Madonna and the duo Clipse. As if this wasn't enough, Williams' band N.E.R.D. released two more albums, *Seeing Sounds* in 2008, and *Nothing* in 2010.

Nothing was an especially stressful album to record, because the band wasn't happy with the original tracks. After recording twenty songs, band member Shae Haley

Surrounded by dancers, Williams performs at the 2014 Very Grammy Christmas television program, recorded on November 18, 2014, at Los Angeles' Shrine Auditorium.

explained on n-e-r-d.com, "It didn't feel right . . . We'd have had something that the average person probably would've been just as happy with. But we would know. Our core fans would know. It just wouldn't be us." Williams agreed, and he said that the twenty songs "weren't really saying what we wanted to say. They weren't good enough." And so N.E.R.D. went back into the studio and recorded all the songs again before releasing the album.

A venture into a different kind of music took Williams' fame over the top. In 2010, Pharrell wrote the soundtrack for the hit movie *Despicable Me*. Then he wrote several new songs for the movie's sequel *Despicable Me 2*, which came out in 2013. One of the songs was "Happy."

Comedian and talk-show host Ellen deGeneres was on hand to honor Williams as he received his own star on the Hollywood Walk of Fame on December 4, 2014.

The upbeat tune became popular and it reached the number-one spot on *Billboard's* Hot 100 chart. "Happy" was also nominated for Best Original Song at the 2014 Oscars, although it lost to "Let It Go" from the movie *Frozen*. Williams performed "Happy" during the awards show.

"Happy" was only one of Williams' hits during 2013. He also co-wrote "Blurred Lines" with Robin Thicke, and Williams produced and sang the song. The song reached number one on the US music charts, as well as on the music charts in thirteen other countries. Later Williams produced and sang "Get Lucky," co-written with Daft Punk, which also reached number one on the *Billboard* charts and won Record of the Year at the 2014 Grammy Awards.

By 2014, Williams was a worldwide superstar. He released his second album, *Girl*, in March. To support the album, he went on tour in Europe. Williams also appeared as a coach in 2014 on the seventh season of the popular television show *The Voice*. His friend Gwen Stefani joined him. The other judges were Blake Shelton and Adam Levine, and the show proved extremely popular with viewers. Williams found the experience inspiring. "Being on *The Voice* has enhanced my life," he told *USA Today*. "It's just allowed me to pay forward everything that I've learned . . . the incredible suggestions that have been given to me."

> *"Being on* The Voice *has enhanced my life," he told* USA Today. *"It's just allowed me to pay forward everything that I've learned . . . the incredible suggestions that have been given to me."*

Pharrell Williams' love for children was easy to see as he hosted a charity shopping event at Uniqlo's store in Los Angeles, California, on December 9, 2014.

CHAPTER 5

The Real Pharrell

Over the years, Pharrell Williams has been a tremendous force in the music industry. As his fame grew, he also lent his time to organizations that work to make the world a better place.

Williams believes that getting young people to vote is one of the most important ways to make people's lives better. On a 2004 MTV broadcast Williams and hip-hop star P. Diddy urged young people to vote in that year's presidential election. Williams is also concerned with how people treat animals and in 2004, he worked with People for the Ethical Treatment of Animals (PETA). Williams recorded an answering-machine message that people could download from PETA's website encouraging listeners to check out PETA's website and be kind to animals.

Ever since 2004 Williams has given back to his childhood community of Virginia Beach by donating money to back-to-school supply drives and food distribution programs. In 2008, Williams founded an organization called From One Hand to AnOTHER (FOHTA). FOHTA's goal is to provide the tools children need for success. Their website explains that during Williams' childhood, "Times were tough but his family was strong and he was lucky enough to find his tool for the future: music. That discovery changed his life and is the reason he is successful today. Pharrell credits his music teacher [for] helping him make something of his gift, teaching him discipline, and never giving up on him."

> **The Arby's restaurant chain submitted the winning bid of forty-four thousand dollars, and Williams donated all of the money to fund FOHTA's summer camp programs.**

Williams believes that if all young people had access to programs that helped them find their passions, they would hold the key to successful futures. Williams has focused FOHTA's programs in the areas of science, technology, engineering, arts, mathematics, and motivation and FOHTA has partnered with NASA to create local space camps for the youth of Virginia Beach.

In 2014, Williams came up with a unique way to raise money for FOHTA. He wore a large, brown hat to the Grammy Awards. The hat quickly became famous, and Williams decided to auction it off on eBay. The Arby's restaurant chain submitted the winning bid of $44,000, and Williams donated all of the money to fund FOHTA's summer camp programs.

In 2008, Williams' longtime girlfriend Helen Lasichanh gave birth to their son Rocket Ayer Williams. Williams wrote the song "Rocket's Theme" for the *Despicable Me* soundtrack to honor his son. On October 12, 2013, Williams and Lasichanh got married on a yacht named *Never Say Never* in Miami, Florida.

Pharrell Williams poses next to a wax figure of himself at Madame Tussauds in New York City.

For all of Williams' success, he is a humble man who does not believe in bragging about material things. Williams told VH1 that young people who want to get into the music industry should understand that success is not about the money. "It's not platinum and diamonds and Mercedes," he warned. "It is business, work, concentration, discipline, and understanding. All those other things, they come along with success, and success is derived from educating yourself."

Unlike many other hip-hop performers, Williams does not brag in his songs. "I don't like bragging," he told *USA Today* in 2014. "It's not about me. It's dedicated to the fan base that put me here. I'm a regular guy. I don't find myself that interesting. I have the same story people have heard a million times."

Williams said that he has trouble thinking of himself as a solo performer. "I never knew I had a solo career because I produce for other people," he told *USA Today*. "I never looked at myself as an artist. Producing means leaving my ego at the door and allowing the artist to shine so I can frame the picture."

Williams has no plans to slow down and he continues to write music for movies. In 2015, his song "Shine" was featured in the movie *Paddington* and he also wrote several songs for the new Spongebob Squarepants movie *Sponge Out of Water*. Williams is also filming another season of *The Voice*. After working with such musical superstars as Justin Timberlake, Miley Cyrus, Britney Spears, Usher, and Jay-Z, it's clear that Williams' and The Neptunes' talents will continue to make new and exciting music in the years to come. Pharrell Williams has many gifts and he likes nothing better than sharing them with the world.

Williams shows his colorful fashion style during the iHeart Radio Jingle Ball concert in Tampa, Florida, on December 22, 2014.

1973   Pharrell Williams is born on April 5.

1980   The Williams family moves to the suburbs of Virginia Beach.

1980s   Williams becomes friends with Chad Hugo.

1992   Williams writes a verse for Wrecks-N-Effect's popular single, "Rump Shaker."

2001   The Neptunes produce Britney Spears' single "I'm a Slave for U." N.E.R.D. releases its first album *In Search Of* in Europe.

2002   *In Search Of* is released worldwide. The Neptunes win Producer of the Year awards at the Source Awards and *Billboard* Music Awards. The Neptunes win their first Grammy Award.

2003   Williams releases his first solo single "Frontin'" featuring Jay-Z. The Neptunes release their album *The Neptunes Present . . . Clones.*

2004   N.E.R.D. releases its first album *Fly or Die.*

2005   *Esquire Magazine* names Williams the Best Dressed Man in the World. He starts the clothing labels Billionaire Boys Club and Ice Cream.

2006   Williams releases his first solo album *In My Mind.*

2008   Williams creates the organization From One Hand to AnOTHER (FOHTA) to help youth. His son Rocket Ayer Williams is born. N.E.R.D. releases the album *Seeing Sounds.*

2010   N.E.R.D. releases the album *Nothing.* Williams writes songs for the movie *Despicable Me.*

2013   Williams writes several songs for the *Despicable Me 2* soundtrack, including the hit "Happy." He produces and performs the hits "Blurred Lines" and "Get Lucky." The song "Happy" is used to create the first twenty-four-hour interactive video. Williams marries Helen Lasichanh.

2014 "Happy" is nominated for an Oscar for Best Song and Williams performs the song at the awards ceremony. He releases his second solo album *Girl* and he appears as a coach on *The Voice*.

2015 Williams records "Shine" for the movie *Paddington*, as well as several songs for the Spongebob Squarepants movie *Sponge Out of Water*. He appears as a coach on *The Voice* for another season.

DISCOGRAPHY

The Neptunes
2003 *The Neptunes Present . . . Clones*

N.E.R.D
2002 *In Search Of*
2004 *Fly or Die*
2008 *Seeing Sounds*
2010 *Nothing*

Pharrell Willliams
2006 *In My Mind*
2014 *Girl*

Brown, Terrell. *Pharrell Willliams*. Broomall, Pennsylvania: Mason Crest Publishers, 2007.

Morreale, Marie. *Pharrell Williams*. New York: Children's Press, 2015.

Waters, Rosa. *Hip-Hop: A Short History*. Broomall, Pennsylvania: Mason Crest Publishers, 2007.

Works Consulted

About N.E.R.D. http://n-e-r-d.com/about/

Gundersen, Edna. "Pharrell: Grammy Magnet, Hitmaker, Producer, Hat Fancier." USA Today.com. February 19, 2014. http://www.usatoday.com/story/life/music/2014/02/19/pharrell-williams-oscar-interview-happy/5472773/

Gundersen, Edna. "Pharrell's 'Happy' to Convey a Message People Can Use." USA Today.com. February 19, 2014. http://www.usatoday.com/story/life/music/2014/02/19/pharrell-oscar-song-nomination-happy-despicable-me-2/5472637/

Kirk, Kristen de Deyn. "The First Mom of Music." *Coastal Virginia Magazine.com*. October 2014. http://www.coastalvirginiamag.com/October-2014/The-First-Mom-of-Music/index.php?cparticle=2&siarticle=1#artanc

PHOTO CREDITS: Cover, p. 1—Turkbug/Dreamstime, (background)—Thinkstock; p. 4—Kevin Kane/ Getty Images for iHeartMedia p. 7—Mark Davis/Getty Images p. 8—Kevork Djansezian/Getty Images; p. 12—Larry Busacca/Getty Images; p. 16—Chelsea Lauren/WireImage; p. 19—Frederick M. Brown/Getty Images; p. 20—Axelle/Bauer-Griffin; p. 22—Chris Weeks/Getty Images for UNIQLO; p. 25—Gary Gershoff/WireImage; p. 27—Alexander Tamargo/Getty Images for iHeartMedia.

WORKS CONSULTED

Mandell, Andrea. "Smarter. Faster. More Colorful." USA Today.com, December 23, 2014. http://www.usatoday.com/story/life/people/2014/12/23/pharrell-williams-smarter-faster-more-colorful/20670239

Schilling, Mary Kaye. "How Pharrell and a Cast of Hundreds Got Happy for a 24-Hour Interactive Video." FastCoCreate.com. November 22, 2013. http://www.fastcocreate.com/3022066/how-pharrell-and-a-cast-of-hundreds-got-happy-for-a-24-hour-interactive-video

23 Amazing Facts You Didn't Know About Pharrell Williams. Capital Xtra.com. http://www.capitalxtra.com/artists/pharrell-williams/lists/facts

On the Internet

From One Hand to AnOTHER
    http://fohta.org
Official N.E.R.D.
    http://www.n-e-r-d.com
Pharrell Williams
    http://tumblr.pharrellwilliams.com/
Pharrell Williams Biography
    http://www.biography.com/people/pharrell-williams

INDEX